little book of

yin and yang

little book of
yin and yang

RICHARD LAWRENCE

Thorsons

Thorsons
An Imprint of HarperCollins*Publishers*
77–85 Fulham Palace Road,
Hammersmith, London W6 8JB

The Thorsons website address is: www.thorsons.com

and *Thorsons*
are trademarks of HarperCollins*Publishers* Ltd

Published by Thorsons 2002

1 3 5 7 9 10 8 6 4 2

© Richard Lawrence 2002

Richard Lawrence asserts the moral right to
be identified as the author of this work

A catalogue record for this book
is available from the British Library

ISBN 0 00 714237 4

Printed and bound in Great Britain by
Martins the Printers Ltd, Berwick upon Tweed

To Mum and Dad

With grateful thanks to Tessa Harrow,
Mark Bennett, Ghim Ping Eugene Sia,
Steve Gibson and John Holder for their
expert knowledge and creative input.

Language Note

I have used the modern Pinyin system of Chinese spelling throughout the text rather than the more outmoded Wade Giles system, which was prevalent until recently. Where familiar terms such as Tai Qi and the Yi Jing occur, I have put their formerly used spellings (T'ai Ch'i and the I Ching) in brackets the first time they occur.

The following is a list of seven of the most commonly used Chinese terms with their suggested pronunciations in italics:

Pinyin	Wade Giles	Pronunciation
Yi Jing	I Ching	Ee Jing
Laozi	Lao Tzu	Laowdzer
Tai Qi	T'ai Ch'i	Tie Chee
Feng Shui	Feng Shui	Fung Shway
Qi Gong	Ch'i Kung	Chee Gong
Dao	Tao	Dow
Dao De Jing	Tao Te Ching	Dow Der Jing

Preface

The entire cosmos is composed of two natural, complementary forces: yin and yang. Every thought, every action, every impulse and every manifestation is composed of these two. They are opposing, yet one cannot exist without the other. To understand them is a secret of life; to harness their energies is a secret of living.

Yin and yang are not restricted to philosophy, science, medicine, religion or anything else – they pervade them all. All life is composed of these two contrasting, balancing and equally essential aspects: left- and right-hand sides of the body, male and female, positive and negative polarities of electro-magnetism, day and night – to quote a contemporary song, they are 'like breathing out and breathing in'.

☯ Yin is generally associated with soft, dark, yielding, receptive, feminine, nurturing qualities; yang with hard, light, strong, creative, masculine, inspirational ones. But as soon as you try to categorize them like this, you have lost something. In their very essence they are not definable or quantifiable. As with so much Chinese philosophy, there is an inherent paradox in the yin/yang concept, because wherever you have *one*, the *other* is always present. Hence in the symbol (shown on the cover of the book), the dark part represents yin and the light part yang, but within each is a small circle of the other. As Leonardo da Vinci put it five hundred years ago:

'Everything proceeds from everything else and everything becomes everything, and everything can be turned into everything else.'

This *Little Book* will reveal to you what yin and yang really mean. It tackles the subject sometimes philosophically, sometimes practically and sometimes humorously. It does not speculate academically on the topic, because this by its very nature would be doomed to failure - intellectual certainty too often limits profound realization. So, please don't just read this book with the rational, left-hand side of the brain - allow the intuitive, right-hand side to offer insights as well.

☯ Above all, this book is designed to enhance your life. You will not be able to write a thesis on yin and yang after one read-through. But, if you use it as a guide through the many situations, decisions and life choices you have to face, it will serve as a reliable source book for you. It could be even more than that – I hope it will become a dependable friend.

Introduction

The Chinese Way

The concept of yin and yang has appeared in Chinese wisdom for thousands of years. The first known reference to it appears in an appendix to the Yi Jing (I Ching) in approximately the fourth century BC. The appendix called Xi Ci, which means 'Appended Explanations', states:

'One (time) yin, one (time) yang,
this is the Dao.'

The highly respected Yellow Emperor's Classic of Internal Medicine, which was at one time thought to date back to the third millennium BC, but is now generally accepted as having been written in its present form in the third century BC, puts it unequivocally:

'The principle of yin and yang is the basic principle of the entire universe ... it is the root and source of life and death; and it is found within the temples of the gods.'

The philosophy of yin and yang has permeated the fabric of Chinese culture up to the present day. This is even reflected in the language, with words of opposite meaning often being juxtaposed to mean something different. So *chang duan* – 'long short' – means length; *da xiao* – 'big small' – means size; and closest of all to yin yang, *hei bai* – 'black white' – is often used to mean morality.

☯ The Chinese approach is based on relativity between contrasting elements. Their cuisine is a blend or harmonization of multiple tastes, aromas and textures. Their poetry, art and architecture all strive for symmetry and balance. Juxtaposing opposites is not contradictory to the Chinese – it enables a grasp of the wholeness of whatever is being contemplated.

❂ This is particularly true in traditional Chinese medicine. Its aim is to bring about balance between the patient's body and the environment, as well as between all its individual components. Illness is caused by a deficiency of either yin or yang. Therefore yin foods will be applied for yang conditions and vice versa. Hot foods, like ginger and ginseng, are yang. In balance, they generate energy, improve digestion and stimulate the metabolism; in excess, they exacerbate infections and fevers. Cool foods, like turnips and dandelions, are yin. In balance, they are cleansing and soothing, relieving fevers, blisters and ulcers; in excess, they are mucus-forming and can cause diarrhoea. As with all other areas of life, good health is a result of balance.

The Yi Jing

Balance also permeates the most ancient known Chinese work, the *Yi Jing* (*Book of Changes*). It uses broken and unbroken lines to represent the creative and receptive aspects of life. Depending on the order and combination of these two types of line, different meanings are conveyed in the text. Nobody knows how old the origins of this book are, since its roots disappear into antiquity. According to tradition, it dates from the legendary period before the Xia Dynasty (c.2205 to c.1766 BC) and is attributed to Fu Xi, whose accession to the throne was in 2852 BC. According to scholars, it came into existence during the Zhou Dynasty after c. 1123 BC. The version we have today originated, according to tradition, with King Wen, progenitor of the Zhou Dynasty, and his son, the Duke of Zhou. Generations of sages and scholars have devoted themselves to deciphering and interpreting its mystical and often coded wisdom.

☯ The most notable of these was Confucius who lived from 551 to 479 BC and was actively engaged in affairs of worldly life, advising on matters of human conduct and etiquette, giving moral guidelines and even holding political office for a while. These last two tasks were often as incongruous then as they are today, with corruption being rife among politicians. For this reason, Confucius resigned from political office, but frequently advised a number of rulers during the Warring States Period. According to tradition, he devoted himself in his latter years to the study of the Yi Jing and wrote certain of its commentaries. It is said that he helped to transform it from being regarded as a book of magical practice into a work of philosophical wisdom. It was, in fact, both. Confucius reputedly said towards the end of his life, 'If my life were to be prolonged, I would use fifty years to study the Yi Jing so that I might escape falling into grave errors.' I should add that there are a number of scholars nowadays who dispute that Confucius had any involvement whatsoever with the Yi Jing. My feeling is that he did, but even if he did not, the profound wisdom of this ancient text cannot be overstated.

● Over two thousand years later, the seventeenth-century German mathematician Gottfried von Leibniz called the Yi Jing 'the oldest monument of scholarship'. He recognized that any number could be written using only the numbers zero and one. This is the binary system of mathematics (base 2), which is used in computer technology today. Leibniz took this binary philosophy further than mathematics by regarding the number one as representing God and zero as the void - hence binary mathematics symbolized the creation of the universe from nothing. In 1703, an article of his was published by the French Academy of Sciences about the relationship between binary mathematics and the Yi Jing.

❷ One of the recent champions of the Yi Jing was the twentieth-century psychologist, Carl Jung. His concept of synchronicity – the significance of events which coincide in a way which appears to be meaningful – fits nicely with the idea at the heart of the Yi Jing that nothing happens by chance. The apparently haphazard throwing of yarrow stalks (and later coins) was deemed to produce a destined result. The way the stalks or coins fell picked out a particular combination of lines in the Yi Jing, known as a hexagram, the meaning of which was required at that moment.

Chinese Mysticism

Confucius' older contemporary, Laozi (LaoTzu), was a far more mysterious and reclusive figure, to whom is attributed the classic work of Daoist (Taoist) philosophy, the Dao De Jing (Tao Te Ching). It stresses the importance of the inner life and the delusional nature of outward actions, which are governed by change.

The only reality is the changeless state. The Dao (Tao), which can be translated as 'The Way', is achieved when a perfect balance is achieved between the inner self and its outer expression. In a sense, Confucius was the yang to Laozi's yin: the first, a high-minded spur to honourable and dutiful action; the second, a mystical and a touch humorous invitation to silent contemplation.

❧ The next great figure in the development of Daoism was Zhuangzi, born some two hundred years after Laozi. He saw the universe as a stream in which one state is constantly changing into another. In the midst of this perpetual change is the principle that each action produces a reaction, which preserves balance throughout the cosmos. Could this be something approaching the Buddhist concept of Karma where action and reaction is opposite and equal (as explained in my *Little Book of Karma*)?

Buddhism was to be taken up in China - far more enthusiastically, in fact, than it had been in India, its country of origin. The ancient concept of yin and yang was easily reconciled to the Buddhist doctrine of eliminating duality. In the eighth century, Hui Neng, the sixth and last Buddhist patriarch in China, founded the School of Sudden Enlightenment. He emphasized that anyone could attain this state, whatever their social standing, through immediate realization. It was based on the idea of detachment from the dualities of life, where pleasure leads inevitably to its opposite, pain. Once this detachment is fully attained, there is a complete inner balance, which instantaneously induces enlightenment. Personally, I consider the idea that total detachment can be attained so suddenly a remote possibility. For most people, it takes many lives to attain permanent enlightenment, though it is certainly possible to enjoy a temporary state of higher consciousness instantaneously.

The Modern Way

Several Chinese practices, based on yin and yang, are gaining popularity in the modern world. Feng Shui, which is currently undergoing a revival in the Western as well as the Eastern world, applies this principle to our personal and geographical environment.

Literally, *feng* means 'wind' and *shui* means 'water'. It is a system for linking people to their environment to bring harmony and balance. Yin elements of water and earth are carefully blended with yang elements of sky, hills and prominent shapes. Interestingly, the Chinese term for landscape paintings (*shan shui*) literally means 'mountain(s) and water'. Feng Shui informs us, for example, that one should avoid having mounds or trees blocking the entrance to one's house; the front door should not open onto a sharp bend in a river or a road; and a house should not face angular roofs or sharp corners. If any of these things are unavoidable, steps may be taken to restore balance by introducing specific yin or yang aspects to the property.

☯ Tai Qi (T'ai Ch'i) is a system of martial arts which is used today mainly to enhance people's lives. Qi Gong (Ch'i Kung) is also a practice devised for physical, mental and spiritual well-being. Tai Qi and Qi Gong both use breathing and the harmonious balance and control of the physical body to harness the natural universal energy, known as Qi. Traditional Chinese medicine, incorporating herbalism, acupuncture and other methods, also draws heavily on the balance between yin and yang.

❂ The existence of two balancing forces is also a feature of metaphysics. My own spiritual teacher, the late master of Yoga, Dr George King, taught that truth itself is polarized – hence the mystical symbol for truth of a double-edged sword. He made the following profound statement in a lecture on wisdom – a statement I would recommend as worthy of deep meditation:

'Truth has two poles – it must have in order to balance. At the exact intersecting point of positive and negative lines of mental force, consciousness is produced. Consciousness is capable of that faculty of discrimination which eventually produces Truth.'

On a more practical level, he introduced a healing technique, the *King Technique*, which employs the principle of polarity in the flow of energy from the palm of one hand to the other. The effectiveness of this technique, published in *The Magic of Healing*, has been proved in literally thousands of positive results achieved by healers around the world.

❂ As well as psychology and philosophy, science is moving in an increasingly spiritual direction with things like time travel, invisible matter and multi-dimensional existence being taken out of the realms of science fiction and seriously considered as science fact. The new science, as it moves ever further into the realms of subatomic physics, is dealing all the time with the polarized nature of matter. Electrons and positrons are the yin and yang of atomic science.

 More important today than academic disciplines are everyday methods of enhancing the quality and spiritual direction of your life. Mysticism is no longer something for the meditative recluse or the scholarly ascetic. It is something for all of us, to be applied to everyday life. Today, for mysticism read self-improvement and service to others. Yin and yang can be applied to diet, fitness, stress control, methods of work, personal relationships and spiritualizing the world as a whole.

Ordinary Yin and Everyday Yang

Once you start to realize that all life is a balance between these two opposing, yet inseparable forces, you can improve any area of your life. The key is getting them to pull in the direction you want your life to take. Here are some examples which affect us all:

Health

Diet was always the first recourse in Chinese medicine. As the physician Sun Simiao said in the seventh century AD:

'A truly good physician first finds out the cause of the illness. Having found that out, he first tries to cure it by food. Only when food has failed does he prescribe medicine.'

Foods were prescribed according to the deficiencies of yin or yang in the patient and

the properties of individual foods. Acupuncture, which can now be obtained on
the National Health Service in some areas
of Great Britain, follows the yin-yang balance of the meridians of the body. Physical
exercise and breathing systems were also
based on principles of equilibrium and
harmony. You can apply this to whatever
measures you take to keep fit and healthy
by ensuring a careful balance in your diet
and the exercise regime you follow. Too
much exercise can be as damaging as too
little.

☯ The yin and yang of health also takes place in the mind. The power of positive thinking has been proved within the medical establishment as well as in the mind-body-spirit movement, as have the negative effects of denial. The secret is striking a balance between the two by first accepting that you have an illness and then taking the necessary measures to treat it, while at the same time adopting such a positive approach that you know beyond all doubt that you will (not might) get better.

Prosperity

True prosperity is not measured by your bank balance – it is a state of being. Having said that, many metaphysical thinkers have come unstuck by disregarding the importance of money. It is not of itself a bad thing, in fact it is an enabler. It is only limiting when it becomes an end in itself and a yardstick for apparent success. Really, money is just another form of energy.

☯ Even purely financial wealth is a balance between what you have and how you feel about it. A millionaire who desperately craves to become a multi-millionaire is poor in his own mind. A person of modest means who is content and grateful for what they have is truly wealthy. Like health, prosperity is facing the facts about what you need while at the same time adopting the right mental attitude. The only poverty is not having what you need; the only wealth is an abundance of opportunity to fulfil your destiny.

Relationships

There is an obvious yin and yang in relationships: the need for compromise, the balance between assertiveness and compliance, direction and support, honesty and compassion. This is true not just in love affairs, but in all kinds of friendships, family situations and business partnerships.

☯ The lesson of relationships can be summarized by the old cliché: there is a time to give and a time to take. This is a simple concept, but not as easy as it sounds. Some people are too preoccupied with themselves and want everything to go their way. No relationship is sustainable on this basis, and such people are generally unsuccessful in them. But there are also those who need to learn how to receive from others, not to be too closed down and inaccessible. A positive relationship has to strike the right balance between the two, so that one is giving when the other needs to receive and one is taking when the other needs to give – we all need to do both.

Work

Stress at work has become a feature of modern living – it is a way for people to recognize the imbalances in their life. Generally it means there is too much yang (outgoing action) and not enough yin (inner peace). Nowadays recreational activities, such as watching and playing sport or going clubbing, are often not truly relaxing. The whole ethos of sex, drugs and rock and roll – which, whatever one's moral standpoint, is a fact of modern life – is designed to stimulate rather than relax. Couple this with the increased pressures of working life, travel and pollution and the gains of modern civilization are outweighed by very heavy setbacks.

❂ The answer to this is to find a balance, not only *between* work and relaxation, but also *within* work and *within* relaxation. At work, allowing the imagination to wander in a controlled way, applying lateral thinking as opposed to literal thinking and having periods of quiet reflection as well as intense thought, can all help. Manual workers can give themselves a mental break when they are doing a routine job by letting their minds wander from time to time, again in a controlled way. When you can, take the opportunity to really relax, enjoy nature, rest near water or use the imagination in music, painting, creative writing or some other hobby. Ideally, take up something like Tai Qi, yoga or meditation. These will all restore the yin in an excessively yang-driven world.

❂ Work should never be regarded as an unavoidable evil; at its best, it is the pinnacle of human achievement. Providing you are doing a worthwhile job, it is your contribution to the general good of others. The best work of all is done for no personal reward whatsoever, or even for the gain of loved ones and friends. Then ordinary work, however mundane the task, becomes a noble calling. And the better the cause you work for, the more fulfilling it will become.

The other very obvious key to work is to enjoy it as much as possible. This simple secret is expressed in an old Chinese saying:

'Love what you do and you will never have to work.'

Spirituality

❂ Absence of spirituality is the biggest problem in the modern world, though the fact that you are reading this kind of book may make you an exception. Dr King used to say that the only energy shortage in the world is spiritual energy – solve that crisis and all the other crises will be solved. In the ancient world, spirituality dominated certain civilizations, though not in the right balance. India, for example, placed too much emphasis on the yin of inner development and not enough on the yang of outward practicality and responsibility for others. Yin is personal spiritual evolution, while yang is the expression of spirituality as love and service.

❂ In this day and age, service is the first among equals. While we have the capacity to destroy the planet, when warfare has become potentially more devastating than ever and world poverty is crushing so many people, it could be seen as an indulgence to focus on your own development. But balancing this is the fact that your motivation to serve and help others can only come from enhancing your inner spirituality - neglect that and sooner or later your capacity and will to serve others will also diminish. Inner development will feed and nourish your spirituality; service is its truest expression.

Meanings

Yin means the shady side
of a hill,
And yang means the sunny side.
The one is overcast, the other
is shone upon.
This is a philosophy which is
literally full of
Light and shade.

History

Some say the yin-yang doctrine
was first defined
By Zou Yan in the fourth
century BC,
But the philosophy is much
older than that.
To the mystic, it must be
older than time,
Which is measured in the
interchange of yin and yang.

Yin

Y - Your
I - Inner
N - Nature

Yang

Y - Your
A - Active
N - Natural
G - Gifts

The Mysticism of the Symbol

The circle of the symbol, which is
on the cover of this book,
Represents the beginning
of creation.
It also contains the five mystic
elements:
The yin (Earth),
The yang (Air),
The yin in the yang (Fire),
The yang in the yin (Water)
And the circle itself (Ether).

The Science of
the Symbol

The dividing line between yin
and yang in the symbol
Is not straight but perfectly
curved.
If you extended it you would
have the symbol of a wave.
The ancients understood that
yin and yang combined
To create a flow of energy which
travelled in wave motion.

Understand Your Qi

Qi is the universal life force;
It keeps you alive;
It is the main manifestation
of the Dao;
When yin and yang are in
balance, Qi is at its most potent.

Maximize Your Qi

Breathing deeply enhances
your Qi;
A balanced diet increases
your Qi;
The right exercise magnifies
your Qi;
Positive thinking potentizes
your Qi.

Breathing Yin

Breathing in is inspiration.
According to yoga philosophy,
The deeper you breathe,
the deeper you think.
So make sure your in-breath
is as long as possible.

The Breath of Life

Breathing out is the yang of
expression.
According to yoga philosophy,
your life is measured
In the number of breaths you
breathe.
So make your out-breath as deep
as your in-breath
For a long and healthy life.

12 Yin Foods

☯

Asparagus, broccoli and spinach;
Fish, salt and tomato;
Corn, honey and most fruits,
Almond, beer and water.

☯

12 Yang Foods

❷

Butter, cheese and egg;
Black pepper, garlic and onion;
Leek, potato and most meats;
Walnut, whisky and wine.

❷

Prescriptions

☯

You need more yin when you're:
Nervous, restless, hyper and
anxious.
You need more yang when you're:
Lethargic, breathless, weak
and fatigued.
Adapt your diet and breathing
patterns accordingly.

☯

Travel

Some people travel for the
sake of a change
When all the experience they
need is here.
If they changed first,
They might get more from
travelling.

Inner Space

Never forget to go within.
Whatever you find in the
material world,
It will not replace the riches
of the yin.
True happiness is a satisfied
conscience.

Outer Space

There is no end to the universe.
It is infinite and ever-expanding.
Manifest the yang of creation
in your life
By accepting no limits.

Zero

Zero is yin.
It reduces all other numbers
to naught.
But, like a vacuum, it must
be filled.
Because, where there is nothing,
There is everything.

Infinity

Infinity is yang.
It is ceaseless, endless
and timeless.
Then, because time has ceased
to exist,
It dissolves into nothing.

A Theory of Relativity

☯

Yin energy is relative to
yang energy.
They are totally separate –
But where there is one,
the other is always present.
It's a lot simpler than
Einstein's theory,
But more conducive to
meditation.

☯

Environmental Change

☯

If summer is yang and
winter is yin,
With spring mainly yang and
autumn mainly yin,
Then global warming must be
an imbalance of yang.
The answer is for science
to enhance the yin
By co-operating with natural law.

☯

Wisdom

Being reasonable is yang –
Being intuitive is yin –
Being wise is both.

Flowers

Exponents of Feng Shui
in the garden
Balance the yin and yang
elements of flowers
To enhance the Qi of
their property.
For example, the rose is yin,
The hydrangea yang and the
begonia both.

Colours

Yin is the blue end of
the light spectrum;
While yang is the red.
Towards the middle come the
yang of yellow
And the yin of green.
Purple can be either or both.

Light and Heat

☯

A dim light is yin;
harsh lighting is yang.
Warmth is yang; coldness is yin.
With the right levels of lighting
and temperature,
The Qi will flow more powerfully.

☯

Property Development

@

Ancient Chinese sages believed
that the ideal spot to build
Was at the mid-point between
two neighbouring hills.
At this point they said the
magnetic currents
Of yin and yang combined in
harmony.

@

Yeshe Tsogyel

Yeshe Tsogyel, the eighth-century
Tibetan female teacher
And consort of Guru
Padmasambhava,
Taught that when male and
female energies
Are united and strictly controlled,
A blissful state of awareness
is attained,
Termed the Initiation of
Creative Expression.

I Am

I am yin and I am yang.
I am that which existed before
them both,
And which will continue after
they both dissolve
Back into the oneness,
Which is the I Am Presence.

Healing Polarities

Healing power flows through the
right palm into the left,
Or occasionally through the
left into the right.
There is a yin-yang circuit of
healing energy
Within us all just waiting
to be tapped.

Perspectives

From where I'm standing I can
see clearly;
But from where you're standing
I can't see a thing.
Perhaps we should swap places.

Symmetry

Your body is symmetrical
but not identical;
Your brain is symmetrical but
different;
Your aura is symmetrical
on a good day;
Yin and yang have a kind of
symmetry about them -
They are two different halves of the
same thing.

Equality

Equality of sex, race, colour
and creed – yes,
Equality of attainment – no.
Sometimes yin is better and
sometimes yang.
Eventually, when neither is
needed in creation any longer,
We will all be equal –
But what will equality
mean then?

Politics

☯

If the left wing promotes power
to the people
And the right wing promotes the
power of authority;
Then it is not clear which
category communism, socialism,
Republicanism, conservatism or
any other ism falls into.
Like yin and yang, the one
contains the seeds of the other.

☯

Buddhism

Buddhism is a path of yin; it
emphasizes going within.
Yet it is very successful in the
world of yang –
It's good to have a major
religious doctrine
Which has not been the explicit
cause of warfare.

Christianity

Christianity, at its best,
is a yang path of love
and service;
Yet it has fostered monasticism,
self-purification
And the Gnostic mystical
tradition –
All based on positive aspects
of yin.

East and West

The sun rises in the east and
yin is born;
The sun sets in the west and
yang prevails;
The mystical east is the source
of inner wisdom;
The practical west is the focus
for worldly attainment;
Individually they each lack
something;
Together they have it all.

Less Stress

Most people who are stressed
need more yin:
Meditation, calm music, a green
or blue coloured lamp,
Deep and even breathing,
a bath in rose oil.
But occasionally they
need more yang:
Helping others causes their own
stress to evaporate.

Mars and Venus

Martians are from Mars and
Venusians are from Venus;
Men are mainly yang and women
mainly yin.
Martians and Venusians have
more Qi than we do –
More yin and yang –
Perhaps that's why they can live
on 'uninhabitable' planets.

UFOs

UFOs have been sighted, filmed
and tracked on radar.
But they allow the mystery to
continue enough
To give the sceptics their day.
Personally, I have my doubts
about scepticism.

The Godhead

A yogi stated to my master,
Dr George King,
That he had seen the Godhead;
My master replied, 'Did you take
your hat off?'
The yogi saw what he meant.
The statement was yin: idealistic;
The reply was yang: practical;
The result was both:
enlightening.

Immortality

According to Daoist philosophers,
Immortality was attained by
liberating the yang soul
From the yin body to become part of
the universal Dao.
The secret was doing it!

Blake and Newton

William Blake abhorred
Sir Isaac Newton
For his brilliant use of reason;
Blake was ridiculed in his day
as a lunatic
For his extraordinary power
of imagination.
Today they are recognized as the
greatest scientist
And the greatest artist
of the time.

Wagner and Brahms

Brahms developed the traditions
he had learned;
His contemporary, Wagner,
relentlessly broke new ground.
Two giants from Germany at
opposite ends
Of the musical spectrum.

Landscapes

Flat, featureless plains for miles
on end are too yin;
Sharp, angular mountains
without much vegetation
are too yang;
They could both do with water
and trees to bring
The softness of yin and the
shapeliness of yang,
Which help to form the beauty
of Mother Earth.

Holidays

☯

If you're working hard at
making a success of your holiday,
It's not a holiday.
A change may be as good
as a rest,
But that means you have to
change with it.

☯

Sexism

If yin disrespects yang,
or yang despises yin
They lose part of themselves.
It's the same with men and
women.

Politically Correct

Conservatives with a small 'c'
want to preserve the best;
Liberals with a small 'l' want to
change the worst.
They're both right.

Peng-Zu

Peng-Zu, the 'Chinese
Methusaleh',
Was an ancient Chinese adept,
Said to have lived for 800 years
by attaining
A perfect symmetry between yin
and yang.
To do this he devised the Dao Yin
which combined
Deep breathing with minutely
balanced physical movements.

The Yi Jing

The Yi Jing is based on
combinations of yin and yang
Represented by broken and
straight lines respectively.
The ultimate yin is six broken
lines representing:
Preservative, female, nurturing,
still Earth.
The ultimate yang is six straight
lines representing:
Creative, male, inspired,
active Heaven.

Confucius and Laozi

The sage Confucius understood
the world of human conduct;
He taught us the wisdom of yang:
how to act.
His contemporary, Laozi,
understood the reality of
existence;
He taught us the perception of
yin: how to be.
Perhaps they planned it that way.

George King

My spiritual teacher, the yoga
master Dr George King,
Taught that service to others is
the key practice today.
He also taught techniques to
realize your inner potential.
Development and service are the
yin and yang of evolution,
But service is the greatest yoga
in these days.

The Picture

It's the big picture –
what you do for others –
That really counts.
The small picture –
what you do for yourself –
Doesn't really matter.
Or does it?
The small picture affects the
big picture
And vice versa.
Maybe there's only one
picture really.

Karma

Karma is a law of opposites,
Expressed through action and
reaction.
So is the Dao,
Expressed through yin and yang.

The Flow

Confucius, standing on the banks
of a river, said:
'Everything flows on and on like
this river,
Without pause, day and night.'
There's a time to go
with the flow –
And a time to change direction.

This and That

☯

This subjective yin approach
Tells you what you really
experience.
That objective yang approach
Tells you how valid your
experience is.
You need both.

☯

Electronics

Electronics is based on
yin and yang.
The positive pole is yang and
the negative pole yin.
Electricity is the Qi.
You need both poles to get
it flowing.

Sport

The team that wins the match
Doesn't always win the game.

Prayer

☯

Prayer is a transmission of energy
Through the person praying
To the object of the prayer.
It is an outward yang expression
of an
Inner yin feeling of universal love.
That's why it's good for the soul.

☯

Fundamentalism

Fundamentalists think only their
way is right.
They're wrong:
The way is right.

Identity

Yang: I think therefore I am.
Yin: I am therefore I think.
The bottom line:
I think and I am.

Possession

☯

If what's yours is yours, what's
mine is mine.
But if what's mine is yours, then
what's yours must be mine.
Possession may be nine-tenths of
the manmade law,
But it's no part of the real law.

☯

Doing Unto Others

'Do not do unto others what you
would not they should
do unto you,' said the sage
Confucius.
'Do unto others as you would
have them do unto you,'
said the Master Jesus.
Two sides of the same coin.

Beauty

Physical beauty is in the eye of
the beholder;
Personal beauty is in the mind's
eye of the beholder;
Spiritual beauty is in the third
eye of the beholder.

Mother Earth

She is the preserver of life.
She could live without us –
But we could not live
without Her,
So She must be greater than
all of us.

The Mighty Sun

It is the source of life.
It provides the energy
for all experience:
The ability to think, to act,
even to pray.
This makes Sun worship far
from primitive.

Lord Buddha

☯

Buddha taught us that too much
of one thing
Leads inevitably to its opposite –
like pleasure and pain.
If you don't believe him, visit a
drugs clinic.

☯

Akhenaten and Nefertiti

Akhenaten and Nefertiti
re-introduced the One God
to Egypt.
This was a great, albeit brief,
achievement of their union.

Crop Circles

Hoaxed crop circles serve a
good purpose:
They show how much better the
genuine ones are.
Fakes prove nothing except the
value of truth.

The Stars

☯

Before you read your stars
in the paper,
Which are based on your
astrological sun sign,
Make sure you know what your
moon sign is too.

Real Art

Classical artists struggled to
reproduce things as they were
In the interests of realism.
Impressionists sought to reflect
things as they looked
For the same reason.
Art lovers find reality in both.

Music

From the freedom of the Baroque
Came the rigid structure of the
Classical,
Leading to the heart-led
Romantic,
Followed by the mentally-driven
avant-garde.
Yin and yang are in there
somewhere.

Dead or Alive

Death is just the beginning
of a new life.
If you don't believe me, ask
someone who's died.

Water and Fire

Sacred water has been used in
many religions;
So has a holy flame.
They can take you to heaven –
and bring heaven to you.

Tragedy and Comedy

The Greeks used tragedy
to purge the emotions,
And comedy to educate the mind.
They were entertaining,
but not entertainment.

Socrates

☯

Socrates was a philosopher
of sufficient yang
To stand up for his beliefs –
and even to die for them.
Fortunately, his student Plato
had sufficient yin
To preserve them for posterity.

☯

Lucky for Some

We use a twelve-month calendar,
Based on the Earth's revolutions
around the Sun.
The Druids follow a thirteen-
month calendar,
Based on the moon's revolutions
around the Earth.
It's lucky they aren't
superstitious.

Twin Souls

☯

We all have a twin soul of the
opposite sex.
When we will meet – in this
or a future life –
Depends on our Karma.
But it will happen at
the right time.

☯

Coming and Going

They say that what goes around
comes around.
That way things get
balanced out.

The Other Side

Life is dual-poled: we exist
in the physical
And the psychic worlds
simultaneously.
Your body is a reflection
of your aura,
And your aura is affected by
the condition of your body.

Great White Brotherhood

The Great White Brotherhood is
a misleading name
Since it is an order composed of
ascended male and female
Masters of whom very few
are white.
They have attained the heights
of spirituality
And work together in love
and harmony.

The Spiritual
Hierarchy of Earth

☯

This is another name for the
Great White Brotherhood.
These masters, who inhabit
ageless bodies,
Form an ordered structure based
not just on ability,
But on their degree of personal
evolution.
This does not have to be enforced –
it is their common will.

☯

Guru and Disciple

The guru teaches the disciple;
The disciple serves the guru;
Enlightenment is spread.

Bacon and Shakespeare

Sir Francis Bacon was
profoundly inspired;
Shakespeare was a brilliant actor
in career and in life.
What can be said about
their plays
Which has not been said before?
Only that a yang production
always needs yin at its heart.

Mary Magdalen

From being a prostitute,
She became a disciple and female
companion to
One of the greatest masters ever
to walk the Earth.
Yin is not limited by social
stereotypes.

Saint Joan

Saint Joan's immense courage
came from
The strength of her yang;
Her loyal devotion came from
The strength of her yin.

Falling in Love

Those not ready to meet their
twin soul in this life
May still find the right person
for balance and partnership.
They might even fall in love in
the process!

Extroverts and Introverts

Extroverts can be over the top;
Introverts can be too withdrawn.
But it doesn't really matter
which you are
As long as you are you.
Balancing out the
yin and yang energies
Will take care of everything else.

Confidence

For confidence, develop the
dynamic yang energies.
These will bring out the natural
yin in you.

Choosing Your Company

There's a time for companionship
And there's a time to be alone.
If you're only happy doing
one of them,
You need to spend time
on the other.

Pressures of Work

We all need to take a break from
the pressures of work
From time to time.
But having to take a break
because there is no work
Can be stressful too.

A Rock and a Hard Place

If you find yourself between a
rock and a hard place,
You are in an excessively yang
situation.
Be like water flowing from one
to the other,
Allowing the yin to clear
your way.

Thinking and Acting

❂

I won't say think before you act,
Because it's impossible to do it
any other way.
Every act was a thought –
And every thought is an act.

❂

Duty

Do your duty when
you're called to –
Because you're needed.
Do the right thing even when
you're not called to –
Because you want to.

Peaceful Waters

Meditate by lakes and rivers to
Become one with your divine
nature.

Holy Mountains

Go to hills and mountains to
Send out spiritual power to the
world.

Victory through Surrender

☯

According to Laozi,
surrender is victory.
Surrender to nothing or no-one
except the divine;
Then it's not really surrender –
it's wisdom.

☯

Decisions

When you know what to do,
But you don't like the feedback
you're getting,
Redouble your efforts
with yang energy.
If you're not sure whether
you're right,
Flow with yin energy
until you know.

Without Religion

☯

In a world without religion
Atheists would have nothing to
disbelieve.
Beliefs may be imperfect, but
they are a link with the reality
Which some people call God.

☯

The Way

I did it my way – it didn't work
for them;
I did it their way – it didn't work
for me;
I did it the way – and found it
was my way all along.

Appendix

❷

Breathing for Harmony and Balance

Here are two breathing exercises for drawing the yin and yang energies to you. Please do not underestimate their powerful effects because of their simplicity.

❷   The Ancients taught that the science of breathing contains the secret of life. By isolating the inner, psychic channels by only

❷

breathing through the left or right nostril, you can determine which quality of energy you choose at a particular time. The goal is to draw the universal life forces (Qi) into your whole being.

❂ You can apply this principle to breathing in the Qi as yin or yang energies by using the following exercises.

Exercise 1: Yin Energies

Block the right side of the nose with your right thumb and breathe in and out through the left nostril for a few minutes. This is a good exercise to do in the daytime when these energies are less accessible and therefore more needed for balance. It can be done at any time to suit you, but especially when you feel the need for yin qualities.

❂ You can potentize this practice by visualizing white light entering you on the in-breath and thinking the following affirmation:

'I AM NOW BATHING MYSELF
IN THE LIGHT OF PEACE.'

Exercise 2: Yang Energies

Block the left side of the nose with your left thumb and breathe in and out through the right nostril for a few minutes. This is a good exercise to do at night when these energies are less accessible and therefore more needed for balance. It can be done at any time to suit you, but especially when you feel the need for yang qualities.

❂ You can potentize this practice by visualizing white light entering you on the in-breath and thinking the following affirmation:

'I AM NOW CHARGING
MYSELF WITH THE POWER
OF LOVE.'

Enhance Your Life through Yin and Yang

When you feel out of sorts, you can apply the principles of yin and yang. You can resolve your inner balance through these two visualization exercises.

When You Feel Mentally Drained and Depleted (Excessively Yin)

Close your eyes. Place your right hand on your solar plexus centre (stomach area) and your left hand on top of your right hand. Breathe deeply and evenly and, as you do so, visualize white light entering you on the in-breath. On the out-breath, visualize white light travelling down through the arms and palms of the hands into the solar plexus. The solar plexus is the location of the chakra or psychic centre which stores your natural energy. It is virtually your battery centre. This is essentially a yang exercise, though you will also receive yin energy if you need it – you will literally be charging up your batteries.

When You Feel Nervous and Hyper (Excessively Yang)

Sit on a hard-backed chair with the palms of the hands facing downwards on the knees. Close your eyes and allow your thought to wander without letting your mind go blank. You should try to observe your own mind. Make no effort, at first, to direct your thoughts – just let them go where they want to. Breathe as deeply and evenly as possible while you do this. After a couple of minutes, visualize your favourite location near water. You are alone there with just nature for company. It may be somewhere you know, or just somewhere that you would love to be. Make sure that the water – whether lake, stream, river or ocean – is completely calm. Try to **hear**, **smell** and **feel** the atmosphere around the water, not just picture it. Then detach from this visualization, open your eyes and mentally return to the room you are in. This is essentially a yin exercise, but yang elements may be introduced where necessary.

Meditate on these words of Laozi from the Dao De Jing:

'Much speech leads inevitably to silence.'

May you experience the yin of peace.

☯

May you express the yang of love.

☯

Richard Lawrence frequently presents
lectures and workshops at:

The Inner Potential Centre
36 Kelvedon Road
London SW6 5BW

Telephone: 020 7736 4187
Website: www.innerpotential.org

Further information from:
Website: www.richardlawrence.co.uk
Email: whatsup@richardlawrence.co.uk